LH
942.719

D1332791

24 FEB 2007		
1 9 OCT 2010		
2 9 MAR 2011		

THE
Old Photographs
SERIES

WARRINGTON

Compiled by
Janice Hayes

CHALFORD

E

First published 1994
Copyright © Janice Hayes and Warrington Borough Council, 1994

The Chalford Publishing Company Limited
St Mary's Mill, Chalford, Stroud
Gloucestershire GL6 8NX

ISBN 0 7524 0040 1

Typesetting and origination by
Alan Sutton Limited
Printed in Great Britain by
Redwood Books, Trowbridge

A shadow of vanishing Warrington – whilst photographing the aftermath of the demolition of old courtyards at the back of Holy Trinity Church, the cameraman also captured his own faint shadow in the foreground.

Contents

Wood's Sweet Shop in Buttermarket Street, near St. Mary's Church. A delightfully nostalgic scene with the old-fashioned shop window, enamel signs advertising Fry's Chocolate, and above all the cosy family group. All was not quite as it seemed, though, for it was not Father who ran the business but the mother, while her husband was a local postman.

Introduction

This volume has been assembled from the extensive archives of Warrington Museum which was founded in 1848, barely a decade after the birth of photography. A vanished world has been recaptured from the images created by amateur and professional photographers alike; coming from family albums, business archives, official records, early newspaper illustrations and popular picture postcards, they all document the changing face of our town.

In 1847 Warrington became a Borough run by its own Council, a body which came to power at a time of national uncertainty, social change, and economic depression. Warrington was not only a thriving regional market town but also a growing industrial centre situated on major road, canal, and railway networks. Soon migrant workers swelled the local population, crowding into hastily built and insanitary housing in the courtyards of the four narrow main streets. New public buildings, houses, shops and wider roads were clearly necessary.

From the mid-1850s the Council planned a series of redevelopments to ensure that Warrington would compare favourably with neighbouring towns, but in the process many old buildings were demolished. In the mid-1850s the Old Market Place and Golden Square were rebuilt. Between the 1880s and the 1900s Bridge Street was widened, followed by Buttermarket Street and the building of a new bridge over the River Mersey in 1910-15. Finally in the 1920s and 1930s parts of Sankey Street and Horsemarket Street were widened before the Second World War shelved plans for further redevelopment. The townscape changed irrevocably and many welcomed the coming of progress – but others mourned the loss of their heritage.

Meanwhile, the cutting of the Manchester Ship Canal had dramatically altered the landscape to the south of the town. Rural communities, traditionally separate villages, found themselves swallowed up to become suburbs of Warrington as the era of the tram and the coming of the internal combustion engine lessened travelling times.

Yet still, the rhythm of the annual calendar continued: schooldays; workdays;

holidays; Walking Days; even harvest time. The Boer War and two World Wars passed by and even royalty came to visit... and always, it seems, there was a photographer on hand to record the event.

Today photographs are commonplace. They bring images of the royal family, the rich, the famous, and the newsworthy from Britain and across the world to the breakfast table via the daily newspaper or the television screen. Almost everyone has access to a camera and increasingly no family event is complete without a video recording. How different from our early nineteenth-century ancestors, who only saw royalty pictured on a coin, learned of major international events days after they had happened, and could not afford a painted portrait of themselves.

The invention of photography in the mid-nineteenth century and especially the emergence of the professional photographic studio had a major impact. It brought our ancestors face to face with themselves, and it allows us to see them as they were, pictured in family portraits, on schooldays, wedding days, at their workplace, or at leisure; or merely caught as curious spectators – watching the photographer recording the scene for posterity.

Bridge Street near Friars Gate, 1897, by Thomas Birtles.

One

Photographing
Warrington

A postcard view of Sankey Street, looking towards Market Gate, mid-1920s.

Bewsey Old Hall, early 1850s, by Thomas Davies (1832-1880). Possibly the earliest and certainly the most artistic of Warrington's photographers, Robert Davies was the son of a wealthy local industrialist and the younger brother of Thomas Davies, founder of the well-known firm of local solicitors. Although he possessed the true artist's eye for composition, Davies was equally fascinated by the scientific aspects of photography, experimenting with a number of the new techniques which were introduced during the 1840s and 1850s.

A 'Calotype' portrait by Thomas Davies, c.1850. This rare portrait was made by the calotype method pioneered by William Henry Fox Talbot in 1841, using a paper negative. Davies' subject might well have had to pose for fifteen to twenty minutes and so not surprisingly he concentrated on landscape photography!

Reverend and Mrs Quekett, *c*.1858. Quekett had become Rector of Warrington in 1854 and immediately plunged into parish work. In 1857 he was advised to holiday abroad for the sake of his health and he 'purchased a complete set of photographic apparatus' en route.

Scene at the old Parish Church, *c*.1858. Quekett continued his hobby on his return from Rome, seemingly allowing his curates to try out the new process. Rebuilding work on the Parish Church began in 1859, a few months after this view was taken.

Studio portrait of William Fell, taken in the 1860s. Himself a talented amateur photographer, Fell was pictured in the studio of John Longshaw, posing with a typical wet-plate studio camera of the period. The print was by now made from a glass negative coated with collodion (guncotton coated in ether) which had to be developed immediately after exposure.

Industrial scene at Bank Quay by William Fell in the 1870s. This site was soon to see massive redevelopment as Crosfield's soap works was extended — doubtless the reason for the photograph since the Fell family had been early investors in the firm.

Warrington Bridge looking towards Bishops Wharf by William Fell, 1870s. Already the growing industrialisation of the town centre was evident, and increased traffic would soon lead to demands to widen this three-arched Victoria Bridge.

General Buller leaving the Town Hall after unveiling the memorial in Queens Gardens, February 1907. This photograph was taken by John Hatton Kertland. During the latter years of the nineteenth century and the first decade of the twentieth, Kertland enthusiastically recorded events of major local significance. His camera captured the scenes of rejoicing which marked the return of Warrington troops from the Boer War and a series of royal events from 1909-11, but with more spontaneity than earlier amateurs. He used a smaller and more portable camera than his predecessors which enabled him to take shots from a moving tram. He was also a member of the Warrington Photographic Society which has produced countless other skilled local photographers.

The hallway at Underclyffe, T.J. Downs, c.1900. Another keen amateur, Downs later turned his darkroom into a practice room for his orchestra but he first found time to take some rare interior shots of a typical upper-middle class Victorian house.

Warrington's horse-drawn fire engine on parade, c.1912, by Harold Shirtcliffe. A typical Shirtcliffe shot from an upper window, capturing a moving procession. By profession the proprietor of a music college, he also found time to record both daily life and special occasions at the time of the First World War.

Samuel Mather Webster as Mayor of Warrington (1875-77), photographed by his son G. Watmough Webster. An enthusiastic amateur artist and a chemist by trade, S.M. Webster had the ideal background to become Warrington's first professional photographer. By March 1855 an advertisement in the *Warrington Guardian* revealed that his premises at 33 Bridge Street could supply photographic equipment and chemicals, while Webster himself took portraits 'plain or coloured' (i.e. hand-tinted). He continued to trade as a 'photographic artist' throughout the 1870s but by the time of his death he was better known as a prominent figure in local government.

Laying the foundation stone of the Warrington Museum, September 1855, S.M. Webster. This picture forms part of a series of 'photographic views' of the event which he later sold at three shillings and sixpence (seventeen and a half pence) a set.

Warrington 'Carte-de-Visite', 1860s, by S.M. Webster (above) and John Longshaw (below). These small portraits mounted on card measuring three and a half inches by two and a quarter inches were produced in large quantities by commercial studios from the late 1850s to the advent of the picture postcard in the 1900s. Taken by natural daylight they demanded exposure times of one to two minutes in duller weather. Not surprisingly, the subjects often appeared stiff and unsmiling — try sitting motionless for that length of time without blinking or moving but maintaining a natural smile!

A young photographer, portrait by John Longshaw, 1860s. The subject poses with what appears to be all the equipment needed for wet-plate photography, including a portable dark room, which was like a small canvas tent on a tripod. A glass plate coated with collodion was exposed in the camera whilst still wet. Immediately afterwards it had to be developed with pyrogallic acid and fixed with hyposulphite of soda. Since Longshaw's studio did take photographs outdoors this may well have been his own equipment. The young man may have been his son Edward, who worked in the family business.

Right: Portrait of Emma Longshaw, 1860s. Photographed by John Longshaw, her father, a cabinet maker by trade who in 1859 at the age of forty seven opened a portrait studio at 34 Sankey Street. Emma was an assistant in the firm but it was her future husband, Thomas Birtles, who was eventually to take over.

Below: Thomas Birtles (1832-1914). Destined to become Warrington's foremost professional photographer, Birtles had begun as a cabinet maker before training at the School of Art. Deciding that he could see a future in photography he began business in Northwich where he had a studio and shop — 'the first premises in Cheshire of a permanent nature for photography'. In 1878 he opened a branch studio in Warrington and by 1881 had moved into the Legh House Studio. From here his reputation grew until in 1895 he was elected a fellow of the Royal Photographic Society of Great Britain.

Above: Interior view of Birtles' Legh House Studio, 1908. 'The studio is of large extent, completely equipped with all the latest appliances, and provided with an unsurpassed north light, this being indeed considered by experts the best lighted studio in the provinces. Instantaneous photography is here carried to great perfection, as shown in the marvellously fine works turned out in children's portraits and animal photography. ... Mr Birtles, who is ably assisted by his son and two daughters, has complete resources. ... Speciality in cabinet portraits and miniatures. ... The studio is open from nine until dusk.'

Left: John Edward Birtles, 1930s. On his father's retirement from the business in 1908, J.E. Birtles continued the family firm until his own retirement in 1951. He had worked alongside his father and claimed the credit for a number of the studio's most famous photographs.

Monks Hall Steelworks, 13 March 1904, by Birtles Studio. Besides becoming a leading portrait photographer Thomas Birtles won many commissions to record industrial scenes. Whilst still in Northwich the Hammond Electrical Light Company engaged him to record the first salt mine lit by electricity. At Northwich he became acquainted with engineer Edward Leader Williams who was later to commission him to document the building of the Manchester Ship Canal (see page 71). In Warrington his photographs found their way into company archives ranging from Monks Hall to Crosfields.

Demolition of courtyards off Bridge Street photographed by Birtles in the early 1900s. When Warrington Borough Council wanted to record the disappearance of Old Warrington it was Birtles' studio which was given the commission. These scenes around Dolman's Lane are reminiscent of the pioneering documentary photographs taken by Thomas Annan of the slums of Glasgow in the 1880s, combining artistry with realism.

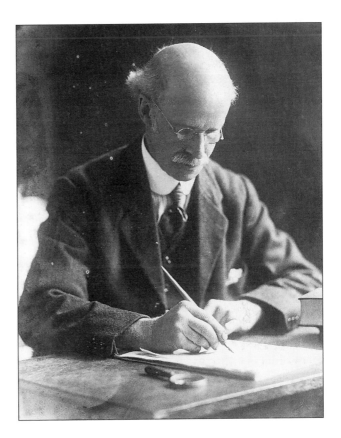

James Parkinson (1862-1932). Birtles' rival, James Parkinson, opened his studio at 45 Sankey Street in 1883, specialising in portraits. In 1925 he formed an association with Messrs Fred Arthur and when the firm moved to Cairo Street in 1931 he traded under the name of Fred Arthur Ltd. From 1934 until 1961 the business was continued by his daughter, Miss Doris Parkinson.

FRED ARTHUR LTD. Photographers,
9, EGYPT STREET, WARRINGTON.

No. P 77392   191

Received from M⟨ ⟩ ⟨...⟩

the sum of ....   Shillings and

Pence for:—

.... Sea **Wave Cabinets**   Photographs will be ready
.... **Genoa Cabinets**
.... **Freda Portraits**
.... **Columbia Portraits**
.... **Sketches**   FRED ARTHUR LTD.,
                                                      PHOTOGRAPHERS,

☞ For the convenience of Sitters the Studio is also
.... but   Per ....
no photos. will be given out on that day.

NOTICE. This Receipt must be brought or sent with any enquiry respecting Photographs.

Parkinsons' brushmakers shop, corner of Bridge Street and Sankey Street, early 1900s. James Parkinson recorded his father's business shortly before its demolition. Together with Houghton's Ironmongers the Parkinsons occupied a part of the old George Inn.

Cabinet Portrait (possibly of the Parkinson family), 1890s. From 1866 until the 1900s cabinet portraits became a popular format for the family album. Sized approximately six and a half by four and a quarter inches, these larger prints allowed larger group shots than carte-de-visites.

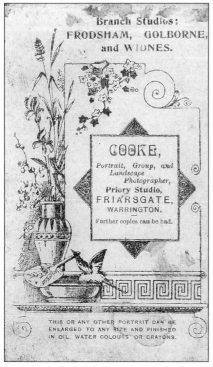

(Above) Charles Cooke's studio, Friars' Gate, from a photograph by Walter Compton taken in the early 1900s. Another of Warrington's studio photographers at the turn of the century, Cooke was more affordable to the working classes than Birtles. This view was taken to record the building which had been the first home of Warrington Museum and Library in 1848 and which Cooke was then sharing with the Independent Labour Party. Note the lamplighter at work on the left.

(Left) Reverse of a carte-de-visite by Cooke. This is typical of many of the elaborate photographers' trade cards of the period, many of which even featured cherubs operating the camera.

The Eagle Printing Works, early 1900s, by Walter Crompton. Crompton recorded his own printing works before its demolition, including his staff and his editor, Arthur Bennett (second on the right). Bennett published a short-lived magazine in the 1900s which featured his crusade to preserve and beautify the town and included several of Crompton's pictures. Unwittingly Crompton became Warrington's first photo-journalist and also documented many obscure back alleyways.

Forrest Street and Knutsford Road, Latchford, by H.E. Tonge, early 1900s.

Tongue's corrugated iron studio in Forrest Street was hardly on a par with Birtles' plush premises but from it he produced many postcards of local news stories. Tonge later became a professional newspaper photographer working for the *Warrington Examiner* until he and his family emigrated to Australia in October 1912.

Postcard views of Warrington. Above: Buttermarket Street in the mid-1920s; below: Grappenhall Village in the 1900s. In 1894 the Post Office first permitted the use of picture postcards, and by 1914 around 880 million cards were sent annually. Despite the difficulties of photographing street scenes — cumbersome cameras and curious onlookers who moved and spoiled the picture — firms like Valentines of Dundee flooded the market until the advent of amateur snapshot photographers in the 1930s.

An unknown Warrington photographer, *c.*1900.

Two
A Changing Town Centre

Umbrella shop off Mersey Street, 1920s.

Bridge Street, c.1855. One of the earliest photographs of the town, this view was probably taken by Bridge Street chemist S.M. Webster. On the immediate right can be seen the quaint bow-windowed frontage of Carters', watch and clockmakers, with the original site of Shaw's butcher's shop next door but one. All the premises featured were about to be demolished to make way for a new draper's shop, later known as Hancock and Wood.

Warrington Policeman *c.*1860, possibly by Webster. Then known as a 'Peeler' (after Robert Peel, a former Home Secretary) this constable was pictured in the early 1860s shortly before a new protective helmet replaced the traditional top hat. One of only nine officers patrolling a town of about 24,000 inhabitants, he was based at the Bridewell in Irlam Street (see page 68).

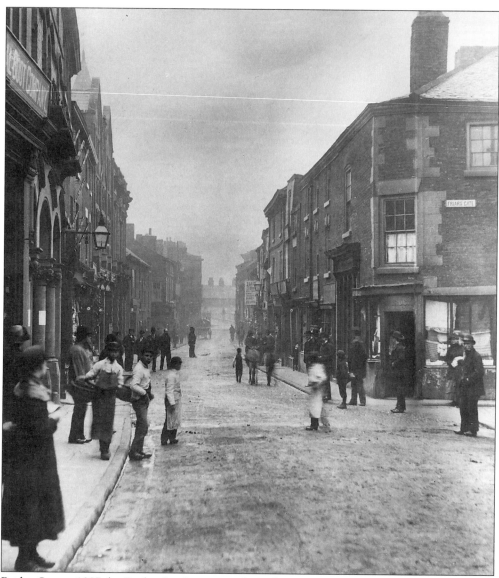

Bridge Street, 1887, by Birtles. Looking towards Bridge Foot from near Friars Gate (right) this shot was taken to record the last days of the old narrow winding thoroughfare before all the west side of the street was demolished to create a new, wider road.

Bridge Street from Warrington Bridge, late 1890s. In the centre of the picture are the newly-built shops with Tower Buildings. On the left is the old Academy which was revealed by the demolition of a building in Bridge Street.

Bridge Street, early 1900s. A close up of Tower Buildings (on the left), then occupied by Greenalgh's Cabinetmakers. A few doors away were the early premises of Boots the Chemists.

The corner of Bridge Street and Sankey Street, 4 April 1905. On the near left stood Olivers' boot shop, Cramptons' grocers and Shaws's butchers. By 1908 all these premises would have disappeared and Alderman Arthur Bennett was so exasperated at the failure of others to catalogue all the ancient landmarks that he commissioned Walter Crompton to make a painstaking record of 'Vanishing Warrington'.

Demolition work in Bridge Street pictured on 22 May 1907 by Crompton. The width of the new street is now clearly visible and Cramptons' grocers continues to trade despite the supporting buttresses!

The corner of Bridge Street and Buttermarket Street, 31 March 1908, by Crompton. As rebuilding of the west side began, the shops opposite had a few years' grace before they too would be demolished (including the old premises of Singletons' butchers, second on the right).

Market Gate on 16 June 1904, by Crompton. The traditional site of Warrington Market and the crossroads of the four main streets, this view has completely altered today. Seen from Bridge Street looking down Horsemarket Street, Briggs and Company stood on the corner of Sankey Street and Horsemarket Street (today the location of Golden Square shopping centre). To the right can be seen the Union Bank on the corner of Buttermarket Street and Horsemarket Street.

The corner of Buttermarket Street and Horsemarket Street, c.1910. A Birtles' photograph recording the scene before the demolition of the old Maypole Dairy (on the right).

Market Gate, *c.*1904 (Crompton). A view down Sankey Street taken from Buttermarket Street. The premises then occupied by Briggs & Co. disappeared when this corner was widened in the late 1920s.

Sankey Street, 1901. A scene of celebration to welcome home local troops who had served in the Boer War, this picture was taken from near the corner of Legh Street looking towards Market Gate.

Sankey Street at the junction with Legh Street, *c.*1900. Only a solitary handcart in front of Neuberts' opticians and the Old White Hart Hotel hints at the increased volume of traffic to come by the 1920s.

Sankey Street between Golborne Street and Legh Street, 1928. Showing right to left: Riley's Game Dealers, Brown's Hairdressers, the old White Hart Hotel and the Winmarleigh Cafe. In 1928, all were demolished to remove a traffic bottleneck.

Entrance to the former Eagle and Child yard from Rylands Street, early 1900s. Later this would be known as Barbauld Street — or more popularly as the back entrance to Woolworths.

The Eagle and Child inn off Bridge Street, early 1900s. The alleyway on the left of the picture led to the inn's Bridge Street entrance which faced Dolman's Lane (now the approach to Warrington Market).

Parr Hall, Palmyra Square, in 1895. The Hall was presented to the town as a public hall at a cost of £8,000 by local banker J. Chorlton Parr of Grappenhall Heyes. The gardens in Palmyra Square (extreme left) were still privately owned but were acquired by the Borough to celebrate Queen Victoria's Diamond Jubilee in 1897.

The opening ceremony at the Parr Hall, 1895. In the presence of the Mayor, Mr J. Fairclough, the opening ceremony took place on Thursday 26 September 1895. In the background the choir and the organist wait to perform Handel's oratorio *Judas Maccabeus*.

The Empire Picture House in Buttermarket Street photographed in the early 1920s. Shown not long after its opening in 1921, the Empire cinema and billiard hall was later overshadowed by a new rival, the Odeon cinema, which would be sited on the extreme right of this view.

The site of the new Odeon Cinema, *c.*1936. The white line marks the extent of the old premises to be demolished to make way for the Odeon — from Wainwright's Yard (to the left of the lamp-post) down to John Chorley's shop. Opened on 11 January 1937 the cinema closed at the end of August 1994.

Buttermarket Street, *c*.1900. Wainwright's butchers shop (on the left) and on the far right, the entrance to Wainwright's Yard.

M. Webb's, tobacconist, 1902. Mrs Webb stands in the doorway of the family business which is patriotically decked with bunting for the coronation of King Edward VII. To the left can be seen the entrance to Wainwright's Yard with the same lamp-post visible opposite.

Horsemarket Street, 26 January 1905. Another of Walter Crompton's records of 'Vanishing Warrington'. The tall building in the background was the old George Inn on the corner of Sankey Street and Bridge Street which was about to be demolished. Several 'vanishing' pedestrians appear in the foreground because of the lengthy exposure required on a winter's day.

Buttermarket Street, early 1900s. One of Warrington's old half-timbered buildings, the former Old Fox Inn, which was shortly to be demolished.

'Tudor Cottages', Church Street, in the 1900s. These three old cottages on the corner of Eldon Street survive into the 1990s because the former neighbouring firm of Rylands (seen in the background to the right) once rescued them for executive dining rooms.

Winwick Street, c.1930. In the days when passengers could still take the tram ride to 'Townsend', past these premises on the corner of Bewsey Street and Winwick Street and on past Central Station Bridge (right).

'Townsend', early 1930s. The old Lord Rodney Hotel on the corner of Pinners Brow (seen on the right). These ramshackle houses were typical of many early nineteenth-century streets of substandard working-class housing at the northern edge of the town.

Three
A Vanished Warrington

The Walker Fountain, *c.*1900.

Warrington Town Hall, Gates and Fountain, c.1905. Erected in honour of Peter Walker, founder of Walkers Brewery, for the then princely sum of £1,000, the green and gold painted cast iron fountain graced the Town Hall lawn from May 1900.

Another 'Walker' fountain in Church Square, Pretoria, South Africa, in 1907. This is one of two other identical fountains manufactured by Walter Mcfarlane & Company of Possil Park, Glasgow.

The fountain from the Town Hall steps, 1915. On a windy day many of the spectators and even some of the passers by in Sankey Street would have been drenched by the spray! In March 1942 the Borough Council made a patriotic gesture by sacrificing the monument to the war effort. The four seated figures of art, science, literature and commerce were tumbled from their pedestals on the forty-foot ground basin by sledgehammers. They were followed by the twelve panels depicting the signs of the zodiac, eight sea urchins (still blowing their horns) from their perches on the upper basin and finally the four entwined dolphins at the pinnacle. Meanwhile the Pretoria fountain survives in the city's zoo — as does its twin in Alexandra Park, Glasgow.

The Old Fox Inn, Buttermarket Street, *c.*1880. Clearly landlord James Hewitt needed to carry out extensive repair work to the centuries' old inn — especially in the face of competition from the newer Crown and Sceptre Inn on its left.

The Old Fox in the 1890s. Spot the difference! Despite the new roof, landlady Elizabeth Earle had conceded defeat, removing the glass lantern from its bracket above the door. Meanwhile J. Murphy, Fancy Draper, had replaced T. Hindley as her neighbour on the right.

The Old Fox's days were numbered, *c.*1912! After closure as a pub, the Old Fox was occupied by a variety of tenants, including Charlie Lee's Oyster shop and R. Lewis' Old Curiosity Shop. Threatened with demolition by the widening of the corner of Bridge Street and Buttermarket Street an attempt was made to preserve the building for posterity.

These were the last days of the Old Fox. As the new buildings tower above it the Old Fox stands isolated with its timbers carefully numbered for re-assembling on a new site. Alas, it spent the First World War languishing in pieces in Victoria Park and the grandiose scheme was eventually abandoned.

Old Buttermarket Street in the early 1900s. During the early 1640s much of the town centre was destroyed in the Civil War. These thatched buildings probably date from the post-war reconstruction and survived until 1936.

'The oldest house in Warrington' pictured in 1905 by Birtles. This one-storey house stood in the angle of Fennel Street and Cockhedge Lane and is thought to date from the early fifteenth century. Built of wattle and daub(sticks and clay) the longer part of the building was probably the great hall and the gable end the family's private parlour.

The remains of the Old Crow, 17 May 1904. Local politician and antiquarian Alderman Arthur Bennett, pictured here in his bowler hat, perches nonchalantly on the crumbling framework of the Old Crow Inn. Without a thought for his safety he observed the lack of nails holding the building together and the fragile plaited wattle panels!

Unveiling the Priestley Plaque on 6 February 1904. The Warrington Society unveils a commemorative plaque on Joseph Priestley's residence in Academy Street from 1761 to 1767.

Sankey Old Hall and Chapel, *c.*1900. Arthur Bennett visits another of the town's ancient buildings.

OLD BARROW HALL & MOAT SANKEY

Barrow Old Hall, early 1900s. A typical picture postcard scene recording another ancient hall which had declined to a farm house. The duck pond was in reality the defensive moat which had encircled the hall.

Appleton Hall, early 1900s. A splendid Victorian mansion, home of the wealthy Lyon family who had made much of their money from land and banking.

Interior view of Appleton Hall, early 1900s. A typically grand Victorian interior, complete with antimacassars and potted palm.

Grappenhall Heyes frontage, early 1900s. This was the home of local banker J. Chorlton Parr whose mansion was considerably more restrained than the home of his business partners the Lyon family.

Grappenhall Hall Lodge, early 1900s. The strategically placed errand boy and small girls in pinafores helped to create a more picturesque scene.

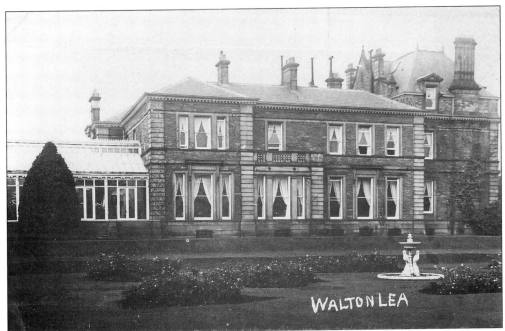

Walton Lea, *c*.1900. This dignified mansion was the home of the Crosfield family who had made their wealth from soap manufacture at Bank Quay. They were Liberals in politics and Nonconformists in religion and thus the rivals of the neighbouring Greenall family who were Tories and Anglicans. When the Crosfields moved away in 1920 the Greenalls bought Walton Lea and promptly demolished it.

Walton Hall, home of the Greenall family, pictured in the 1940s. The Hall and grounds were bought by Warrington Borough Council and put into use as a public park.

The Queen's Hotel, Sankey Street, on 31 January 1907. Formerly a coaching inn known as the Nag's Head the Hotel was renamed in honour of Queen Victoria's Jubilee but demolished in the 1930s.

The Boar's Head Inn, 31 January 1907. This typical small public house stood on the site of the old pig market on Pig Hill, now known as Town Hill.

Tom Paine's Bridge, Stockton Heath, 1890s. This stretch of canal disappeared with the building of the Manchester Ship Canal but quite why the bridge seemed to have been named after a radical eighteenth-century politician remains a mystery.

Ploughing at Penketh, 1902. 'The ploughman plods his weary way' — and was captured on film at Brook Farm by George Bates.

Haymaking near Quarry Lane, Appleton, in the 1900s. This is an amateur photograph of a traditional part of the country calendar taken before the introduction of mechanisation.

Steam threshing at Appleton, c.1900. T.J. Downs documents the beginnings of combined harvesting as the steam engine drives the threshing machine.

Steam threshing at Penketh, c.1900. Brookside Farm owned its own threshing machine but it was clearly still a labour intensive process.

The arch that never was! July 1909. Amateur photographer J.H. Kertland captured the extensive preparations for the visit of King Edward VII and Queen Alexandra on 6 July 1909. Not only were all the main streets decked with bunting but this fake ceremonial arch was put up in Buttermarket Street. Alas, pro-royal fervour was dimmed when the King's car sped past the waiting crowds and he spent barely four minutes at the Town Hall!

Four

Making the News

Local jockey Steve Donaghue visiting St. Mary's School, Buttermarket Street, in 1925 after his Derby victory.

W.E. Gladstone at Bank Quay Station, 1879 or 1885. A landmark photograph of a major nineteenth-century politician. W.E. Gladstone pioneered barn-storming electioneering campaigns and set the fashion of making speeches from railway carriages to enthusiastic supporters. En route to campaign in Scotland in November 1885 he was welcomed by a large crowd of local Liberals at Bank Quay Station at 9.30 in the morning. Many in the crowd had also greeted him on a dark, freezing, foggy evening in December 1879 on his return from Scotland to his home at Hawarden near Chester. Local photographer J.E. Birtles recorded Gladstone's visit — but which? He did take a photograph in 1879, but the weather was poor and he was only sixteen years old. In 1885 Gladstone's carriage was shunted to a quieter spot, probably to create better conditions for this carefully staged 'photo opportunity', so it seems more likely that this picture was taken on his later visit.

The presentation of the Town Hall Gates, 28 June 1895. The scene on the Town Hall lawn on Warrington Walking Day was to become a perennially popular subject for photographers. Here Birtles not only captures the milling crowd of children in the background but also the official ceremony as Frederick Monks of Monks Hall Foundry presents the ornate iron gates to the town.

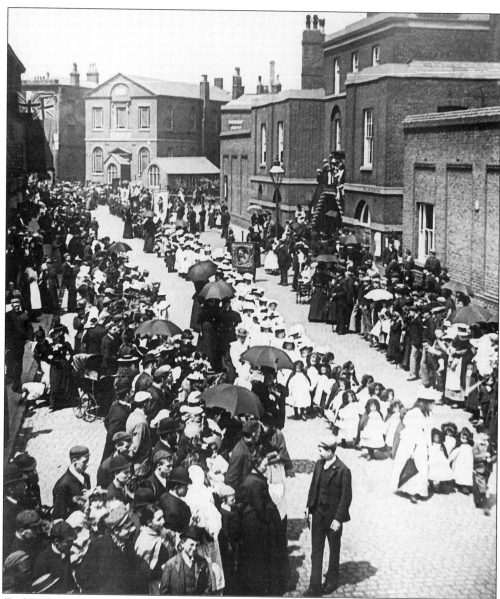

'Red Riding Hoods', 1894. For once the parasols were sunshades and not umbrellas as the Walking Day procession wound its way from the town centre down Buttermarket Street. On the right can be seen the old Bridewell (the police station and lock-up) which would be demolished in 1901 after the new Arpley Street station opened.

Walking Day, c.1894. Spot the difference! The League of the Cross Band leads St. Mary's Church down Buttermarket Street. Unfortunately in his haste to sell postcards of the day the unknown photographer produced at least one back-to-front image. Hold it up to a mirror to see the correct view!

Walking Day, c.1911. Walter Burrell captured this image of Rector Willis leading the Parish Church contingent towards the town centre. Like several other semi-professional photographers Burrell took a number of shots from his vantage point and then issued them as a series to be sold in the windows of nearby newsagents.

Walking Day in Latchford, 1920s. Christ Church band leads the procession past the half-timbered Plague House in Wash Lane. The unknown photographer had found the perfect position to pinpoint the scene and to capture all the atmosphere of the occasion.

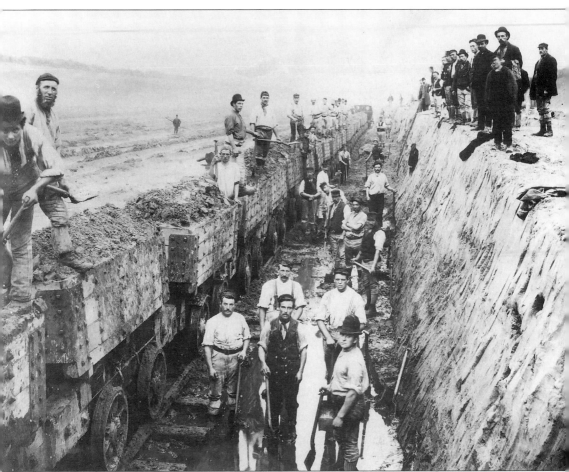

Navvies at work on the Manchester Ship Canal (Birtles). This remarkable photograph is one of the most famous images of the building of the canal — the major engineering feat of the nineteenth century. The construction of the thirty-six-mile canal from Eastham on Merseyside to Manchester between 1887 and 1894 relied heavily on 17,000 navigators (or 'navvies') who shifted 54 million cubic yards of soil and rock. The landscape around Warrington (especially at Stockton Heath) was dramatically altered and the excavations proved an irresistible subject for local cameramen. Thomas Birtles records how he became the official photographer for the entire project: 'I had a free hand from Eastham to Irlam, where all the heavy work was done. My work was the only series of views accepted by the contractors. … I made the set of views and prepared the folio that was presented to our Queen Victoria when she opened the canal.'

The construction of Latchford Locks, Birtles portfolio no. 89. Birtles' studio produced stunning images which not only demonstrated the scale of the engineering project but also the endeavours of the workforce. This, despite the photographers having to clamber over muddy embankments with cumbersome equipment.

Latchford Locks — an amateur view. Still a dramatic image but lacking the technical quality of Birtles' work.

The impact on Stockton Heath — a lantern slide view. On the right is the new swing bridge over the canal and in the centre the curved line of the old London Road arching round towards Greenalls' Wilderspool Brewery.

Warrington dignitaries on board the Helvetia for the official opening of the Manchester Ship Canal on 1 January 1894.

Welcoming home the troops, 1901. Birtles took this remarkable photograph of the crowded scenes in Winwick Street when almost the whole town turned out to welcome home 'the khaki clad heroes' who had fought against the Boers in South Africa. The streets were decked with flags and bunting and a banner was hung in Sankey Street proclaiming 'Volunteers We Are Proud of You' (see page 40). Near Central Station people had planted themselves 'on the housetops, hoardings, walls, electric lampposts — in fact almost everywhere'. No wonder the troops had great difficulty marching back to their barracks in Orford Lane!

King Edward VII's Memorial Service, 20 May 1910. From his vantage point on the Rectory wall, J.H. Kertland recorded the crowds who turned out in brilliant sunshine to watch the ceremonial arrivals at the Parish Church. The whole town had taken the day off to mourn whilst small children perched on the windowsills of Rylands' Wire Works (above) to watch the Territorials and the South Lancashire Regiment (below) march past.

Building Warrington Bridge, 14 March 1914. The present bridge over the Mersey was built between 1911 and 1915 and the Council commissioned the Birtles studio to make a systematic record of the construction work. The Warrington Examiner published some expert hints for amateur photographers in August 1914 recommending a vantage point at Arpley, looking towards Bishops Wharf. 'The softening light of a misty morning makes it well worth several attempts by an amateur at securing a picture … the beautiful double curve of the finished portion makes a worthy foreground to the picture'.

Opposite, above: The official opening of the first half of the Bridge, 7 July 1913. King George V and Queen Mary were welcomed at the Town Hall by an official party which included the designer of the bridge, John James Webster, who was the son of photographer S.M. Webster.

Opposite, below: 'The presentations over, His Majesty, by pressing an electric button fixed on the royal dais, severed a rope stretched across the Northern end of the completed section of the new Warrington Bridge, and the firing of a gun in the neighbourhood of the river announced that the plan had been successfully carried out'.

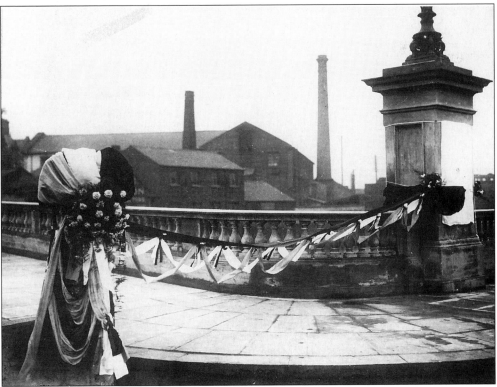

The Royal procession, 7 July 1913. King George V and Queen Mary travelled down Bridge Street in open carriages on their route from Arpley Station to the Town Hall. 'Everybody, young or old, had a good view of their Majesties and this was regarded as ample compensation for the disappointment experienced on the occasion of the flying visit of King Edward VII in 1909' (see page 64).

A commemorative postcard of the 1913 Royal visit. A clear view of the royal couple in one of Lord Derby's carriages, pulled by four dark brown horses which were ridden by postillions in Derby livery.

An amateur view of the 1913 procession. From his vantage point high above the corner of Sankey Street Harold Shirtcliffe captured the drama of the occasion — the moving carriage and the excited, cheering crowd.

The National Railway Strike, 18-19 August 1911. 1911-1912 saw a period of massive industrial unrest and in August 1911 the railway workers went on strike to demand an increase in pay of 2/- (10p) a week and a fifty-four hour week instead of sixty hours. A national state of emergency was declared and at Warrington three hundred and thirty six men and fifteen officers of the 18th Hussars were sent to guard railway property and ensure the movement of essential supplies.

Exercising the railway delivery horses at Central Station (photograph by Walter Burrell).

The launch of the Santa Rosa, Sankey Bridges, 7 July 1906. Built at Clare and Ridgeways' yard for the United Alkali Company, the Santa Rosa was dramatically launched by Mrs Ridgeway. 'The vessel ... slid broadways down inclined planks taking to the water with a fine plunge amidst the cheers of the spectators.'

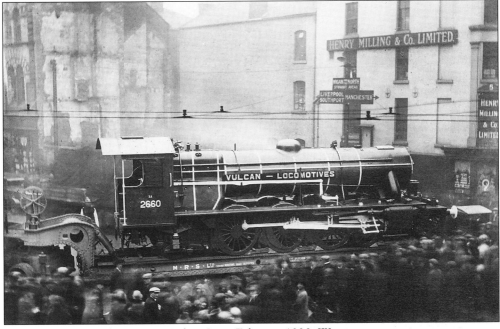

The train now standing ... at Market Gate, February 1930. Warrington town centre came to a halt as this locomotive, built at the Vulcan Foundry in Newton-le-Willows, squeezed through the narrow streets en route to India via Liverpool Docks.

Hot air balloon at Appleton, early 1900s. Amateur photographer T.J. Downs recorded this dramatic event in the life of a sleepy country village

Up, Up and Away! Still tethered to a farm cart the aviator hovers a few feet above the ground, whilst the crowd follows behind determined not to miss the moment of take-off.

Five

Transport

An early Warrington car, c.1900s.

Strange's horse-drawn bread van, pre 1914-18 war. A familiar daily sight from its Knutsford Road depot but sadly driver William Bridge was killed in the First World War.

Ferguson's Forge off Ryland's Street, 1884. In the age of horse-drawn vehicles a blacksmith was in great demand, especially in a busy town centre.

Horsebuses in a blizzard, c.1900. A pioneering photograph taken in a snowstorm, this lantern slide shows two horse-drawn omnibuses in Horsemarket Street. 'Coops Concert Room' was on the corner of Peter Street and is better known as the Hop Pole Hotel.

Pony cart at the Plough Inn, Lymm, 1902. 'Cabby' Wilson on the far left looks on as the driver resists the temptation to have 'one for the road'.

Horsebus at Stockton Heath, *c.*1900. One of the various horse-drawn omnibuses which carried passengers around the town from the 1890s until the introduction of Warrington Corporation's electric tramcars in 1902.

Horsebus at Sankey, *c.*1900. Three horses were needed to pull this top-heavy vehicle pictured near St Mary's Church.

Horsebus at the Mulberry Tree Hotel, Stockton Heath, early 1900s. It would soon be 'all change' at Victoria Square with the arrival of the new tram terminus and the rebuilding of the Mulberry Tree by 1907.

Tramcar in London Road, Stockton Heath, c.1910. The eventual opening of the new tram route from Bridge Street to Stockton Heath on 7 July 1905 encouraged the development of the village as a commuter suburb of Warrington with more of the professional classes moving there from the overcrowded town centre.

Crosfields' Steam Wagon, 1903. From the early 1900s several local businesses began to use steam power instead of horse power for their deliveries. This splendid vehicle could reach a speed of five miles per hour.

Crosfield's fleet of delivery lorries, 1930s. The manufacturers, Thornycroft Motor Vehicle Works at Basingstoke, commissioned their own photographer to record the latest addition to Crosfields' fleet.

Charabanc excursion from the Brooklands Hotel, c.1920. Well wrapped up for a windy ride the regulars pose for a postcard portrait to commemorate their pub outing.

The family car of the 1920s. Ernest Caldwell, Arthur and Dorothy with their Singer car.

Warrington Fire Brigade, late 1890s. Ready for action with 'Captain' and 'Major', Warrington's two Merryweather steam fire engines. Purchased in 1880, 'Major' cost £463 whilst 'Captain', purchased in 1894, cost £520. The horses were borrowed from local owners who were paid a retaining fee plus five shillings (twenty-five pence) per hour for a fire.

Crosfield's Fire Brigade, 1920. A carefully posed photograph, probably by Birtles' studio, showing the works brigade which still retained its steam fire engines whilst the Borough had already begun to acquire motorised vehicles.

London Bridge, Stockton Heath, 1908. Trans-shipping goods on the eighteenth-century Bridgewater Canal which remained a busy goods highway despite the coming of the railways and the development of road vehicles. This original bridge was replaced in 1936 by a wider structure and the canal was left to pleasure traffic.

'A busy time at Latchford Locks', c.1911. This photographic postcard by H.E. Tonge captured the Manchester Ship Canal in its heyday as parents took their small children to marvel at the gigantic ships.

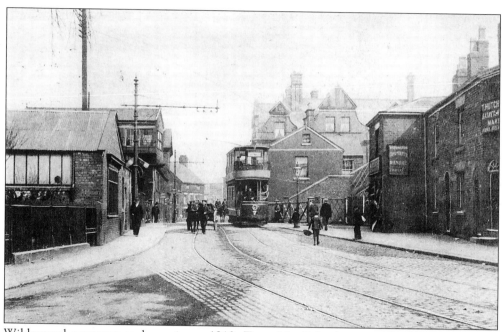

Wilderspool causeway and crossing, *c.*1910. Tram No. 7 lumbers over Wilderspool railway crossing en route for Stockton Heath. Hard to imagine that this tranquil scene would soon become a major traffic bottleneck which was not relieved until the opening of the new Wilderspool Bridge in 1957.

Steam and speed, *c.*1910. A London and North Western locomotive thunders through Wilderspool Crossing with the imposing Norton Arms Hotel in the background.

Latchford Old Station in the early 1890s. The last train from Latchford will shortly be leaving from this platform! The station was to be closed with the building of the adjacent Manchester Ship Canal.

Lymm Station at the turn of the century, a typical rural station with its immaculately swept platforms and enamel advertising signs.

Electricity comes to Lymm, mid-1920s. Installing electricity in sleepy Lymm in the 1920s seemed to cause less havoc than the installation of cable T.V. in the 1990s — but then there was less traffic to disrupt with only a Model T Ford in the background and a Tilling Stevens motor bus which had been sold to the Electricity Company by Warrington Transport.

Six
People in Focus

Teddy Bears' Picnic at Appleton, 1905-1910.

Fairfield Infants, 1924. Carefully posed around the splendid dolls' house the children gaze awkwardly at the camera. Whilst three girls tenderly display the china dolls the custodian of the class teddy bear looks less than delighted with his charge!

Oakwood infants, mid-1920s. Beneath a colourful frieze of nursery rhyme characters the infants are seemingly too absorbed in their activities to notice the camera.

A Stockton Heath classroom in the 1900s. Shining scrubbed faces peer unblinkingly at the camera as rigid class discipline is obeyed and the nature study session is interrupted.

Penketh School, November 1919. Mr Griffith, the headmaster, and class teacher Miss Wynne keep order in this bleak classroom where even the high windows ensure minimum distraction.

Empire Day at Oakwood Junior School, 1920s. On the far left Britannia gathers her multi-national subjects to celebrate the days when Britain seemed to rule the world and national pride had a place on the national curriculum.

Cookery lesson at Beamont School, c.1920. Principles of nutrition and practical food preparation at the kitchen range tried to ensure these future mothers would give their families a healthy diet.

Seven sets of twins at Silver Street School in 1929. Left to right (back): George and Tom Fletcher; Harold and Sydney Wilcock; Tom and Joseph Watson; Tom and Arthur Dennett. Left to right (front): May and Harold Isherwood; Harry and John Irwin; Heather and Sarah Adams.

Thirteen sets of twins at Silver Street School in 1930. Left to right (back): Stan and Henry Healey; Tom and Lily Delooze; the Adams; June and Ben Booth; the Irwins. Left to right (centre): the Dennetts, the Watsons, the Isherwoods, the Fletchers. Left to right (front): Ivy and Olive Dobson; Eric and Leslie Webster; Margaret and Harold Clements; Albert and Florence James.

Girls and boys come out to play! Above: Paddling in Lumb Brook, *c.*1900. Below: 'Slumming with a hand camera'. This documentary photographer captured four young urchins playing in a back street off Winwick Street. Hand-me-down clothes highlighted their poverty and because of the high infant mortality rate all would be lucky if they reached adulthood.

Cabinet portrait of the Throssell family by Cooke and Son, c.1900. Mr and Mrs Joseph Throssell pose with daughter Gladys, eldest son William (right) and young Harold who was seated on an orange-box, which rather destroyed the illusion of rustic grandeur created by the painted backdrop!

High society wedding portrait, *c.*1895. Taken in the conservatory of the bride's home this has all the hallmarks of a formal portrait by the Birtles studio and can be dated by the women's dresses.

Susannah Greenall's wedding at Walton Hall, 7 July 1898. The wedding group, left to right: Bertha Greenall (bridesmaid), Sir Gilbert Greenall (brother), Susannah (bride), Cyril Greenall (bridegroom), J. Whitley (best man), Miss C. Greenall (bridegroom's sister and bridesmaid). And the bride wore: 'a charming dress of white satin embroidered with chenille and diamonds, with a train draped with Brussells lace flounce … and a wreath of orange blossom and a tulle veil'.

Working class wedding, 1914-18. A wedding and family reunion were recorded in the back yard of the bride's terraced home. The floral bedcover draped over the wall was a brave attempt to capture the atmosphere of a formal garden.

The happy couple, 82 Scott Street. Minnie Emery chose a sensible suit for her marriage to collier William Schofield but the day was not without its drama when the bridegroom had to make a hasty dash home to Haydock to collect the marriage licence.

Warrington postman, *c*.1910. Postman 48's uniform helps to pinpoint the date of the photograph since his cap or 'shako' is of the type in use 1896-1910, whilst his knickerbocker trousers and puttees (leg bandages) were introduced about 1910 for postmen with bicycles — and also as a defence against hostile dogs!

Mr Joseph Shaw, Butcher, photographed by Crompton on 4 April 1905. 'The oldest tradesman in Warrington', Mr Shaw continued to serve at his Bridge Street shop until his death at the age of 79.

Scenes of everyday life: Sankey Bridges, 1905. Tom Francis the Bridgeman (pictured second on the left) may have looked like an old sea dog but his wooden legs were the result of an accident on the railways.

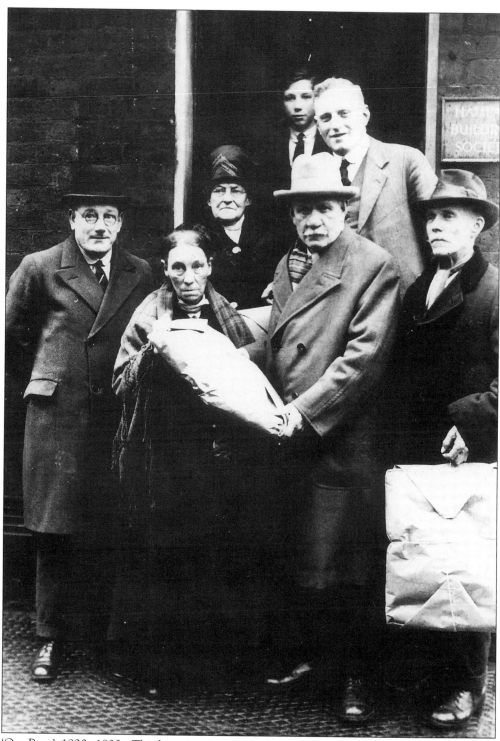

'Our Poor', 1920s-1930s. This human interest story captures the despair and humiliation of the old couple receiving a blanket from Bob Cook (back row, right), who was dispensing charity to the poor from the offices of Gittens and Cook in Golborne Street.

Seven

Warrington at Work

Soap stamping room at Crosfield, 1896.

Rylands' Wire Works, *c.*1900. Warrington and Wire — the association of the town and the industry began by the early nineteenth century, with Rylands soon establishing themselves as one of the town's leading wire manufacturers.

Longford Wire, Iron and Steel Company, *c.*1900. The demands of wire drawing and wire weaving led Warrington firms to set up their own iron and steel works which soon became major employers of the local labour force.

Rylands' steam hammer, *c*.1900. Probably at Rylands' original Church Street works (later the site of Sainsbury's supermarket). With the national decline and restructuring of heavy industry in the 1980s, steel production in the town ceased. The wire trade continued to supply a world-wide market, but with a greatly reduced work force.

Employees of Houghton's Wire Works, Sankey Bridges, *c*.1900. All wear the traditional labourer's costume of cloth cap, collarless shirt and trousers held up with braces.

Large soap pans at Crosfields' Soap Works, 1904. Joseph Crosfield began making soap at Bank Quay in 1815 and his sons and grandsons expanded the business and diversified into industrial chemical production. Crosfields began an extensive photographic archive showing all aspects of the firm which became part of the Unilever Group in 1929.

The Glycerine Plant, early 1900s. By 1913, Joseph Crosfield and Sons claimed to be the largest producers of chemically pure glycerine. By the 1990s Crosfields Chemicals had become one of Britain's major chemical companies, exporting silica-based products world-wide.

Crosfields' main laboratory, 1911. Trained chemists were employed from the 1890s to develop new products and improve manufacturing processes.

Crosfields' general offices, 1896. The world of ledger clerks and cashiers was dominated by men until the arrival of women typists and women workers during the First World War.

Wrapping Erasmic toilet soap 1896. Together with 'Perfection' household soap, Erasmic herb toilet soap became one of Crosfields' best known names.

Surf production line, 1950s-1960s. What a contrast to the 1890s! By the mid 1960s Unilever had rationalised their production, moving Surf manufacture to Port Sunlight and leaving Persil as the major product of Warrington's Lever Bros. plant.

The Alliance Box Works, Orford Lane, c.1914. The bowler-hatted foreman supervises his female workforce who could be producing anything from a cardboard chocolate box to a fibreboard case for a mattress!

Alliance Box workers of the 1940s. Protective overalls and machine guards have appeared since the early days seen above, but otherwise little has changed.

Fustian Cutting Shop, Manchester Road. Warrington played an important role in this North West industry by cutting the pile on specially woven cotton cloth called fustian (or velvet) produced in Manchester. Originally a cottage industry, it was later carried out in a special attic running the length of a row of terraced houses. In 1840 there were about fifty small hand cutting shops around the town. Inside the workshop the cutter would walk the length of a bench which measured twelve to fifteen yards in length, cutting the looped pile on the fabric's surface with a special knife. A cutter might walk as far as thirteen miles in day which lasted ten or eleven hours. Machine cutting was introduced early this century but the industry died out here with the closure of the last cutting shop in Hale Street in 1959.

Warrington mill girls, 1920s. Wearing protective pinafores over their dresses, these two weavers carry the tools of their trade — shuttles and bobbins of thread in their hands and scissors and knives on the belt at their waist.

Cotton spinners at Armitage and Rigby's Cockhedge Mill, 1950s. Unlike many of its neighbours Warrington did not become a major cotton town. At its peak in the 1820s the town had over twenty firms engaged in cotton spinning and weaving but eventually these declined to one mill at Cockhedge. In the 1980s the site was redeveloped as a shopping centre.

Tannery workers de-fleshing hides. Animal hides came from all over the world to be treated in Warrington tanneries and turned into products ranging from shoe leather to belting to drive industrial machinery. By 1937 there were still thirteen tanneries in the town, but increasing foreign competition and cheaper synthetic substitutes killed off this once flourishing trade.

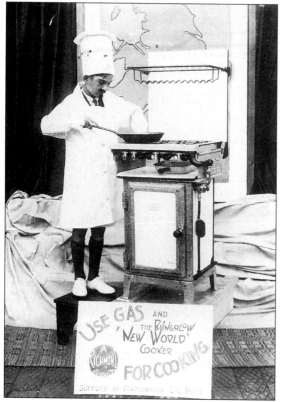

A New World 'Bungalow' gas stove, 1930. A young chef from Silver Street school demonstrates one of Richmonds' latest cookers. The photograph was taken at a pageant demonstrating the wide range of products made by 'The Town of Many Industries'.

Eight
Warrington at Leisure

St Mary's soccer team pictured in the 1900s.

Bawming the Thorn at Appleton, *c.*1910. A reminder that 'holidays' were once 'holy days' this tradition, unique to Appleton Thorn, takes place annually on or about St Peter's Day (29 June) when local children 'bawm' or decorate the tree with red ribbons and floral garlands. The ceremony originated in medieval times when Adam de Dutton, the local lord of the manor, planted a sprig of the Glastonbury Thorn (said to have sprung from Christ's crown of thorns), and was revived in 1973.

Padgate Harvest Queen, 1925. Seated on a magnificent crimson velvet throne festooned with wheatsheaves and surrounded by her courtiers, Florence Mercer, Padgate's first Harvest Queen, was crowned at a fund-raising pageant.

A Warrington scout group, c.1909 — a credit to their founder, Baden Powell!

Penketh Guides, photographed in the Methodist Sunday School yard in 1928.

Bowling at Arpley in the 1890s. Top hats and striped blazers were the order of the day when Birtles recorded this keenly contested match.

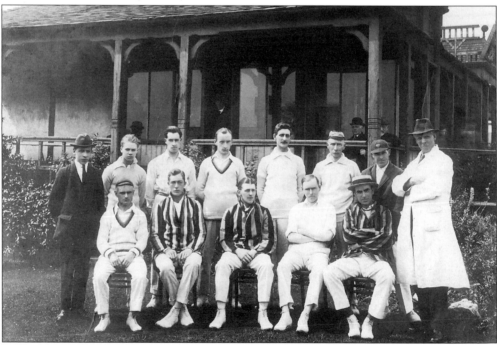

A Warrington Cricket Club Eleven, early this century. Arpley Meadows, scene of Lancashire's first county match, was Warrington Cricket Club's headquarters until the late 1960s when encroaching industrialisation forced a retreat to rural Walton.

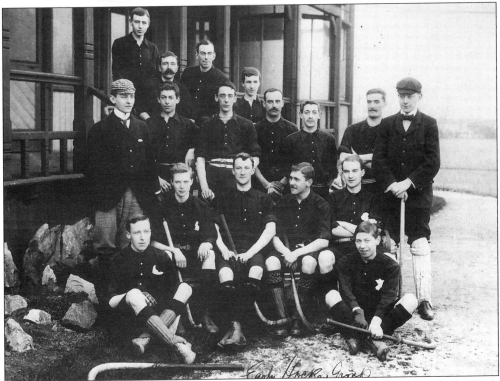

An early hockey team, 1900s. Probably the Warrington Hockey Club, formed in 1893, which shared the Arpley Cricket ground with bowling, association football, lawn tennis, croquet, and rugby union.

Warrington Secondary School's Girls First Eleven Hockey Team, 1900s. Long before the days of lycra sportswear these elegant young ladies glided across the pitch, seemingly unimpeded by their heavy skirts and restricting blouses.

Warrington gymnasium class, *c*.1920. Clad in sturdy gymslips and with newly bobbed hair these modern misses were being coached to keep young and beautiful by exercising with a pair of clubs.

St. Ann's School baseball team, 1930. These young school champions proudly display their trophy for a sport that was enjoying a short-lived pre-war popularity.

Grand Fancy Dress Carnival at the Empire Roller Skating Rink in Winmarleigh Street, Thursday 27 January 1910. 'Over 300 entrants took advantage of the opportunity of competing and the rink was crowded with scores of skaters in original costumes. Dutchmen, colleens, cavaliers, kings, jesters, Napoleons, Kellys, cowboys, lion tamers, saloon smashers and hundreds of other 'make ups' were to be seen ... the carnival was one of the greatest ever held in the country ... '. Amongst the prize-winners was: '"Gent's most Humorous" — 1st. R. Brown, Mrs. Kelly'. (*Warrington Guardian*).

Harriers at Rylands Recreation Ground between 1900 and 1920. Even working men could afford to join this band of cross country runners — although one athlete clearly felt he was above his fellow competitors!

Young Musicians of the Year, c.1910! This motley band of urchins may have lacked string and brass players but at least they had a kettle drum (far left), while a pair of fire bellows made up the wind section.

Crosfields' Prize Band, 1904. Many local firms tried to provide leisure activities for their employees and this works band proved especially successful in competition.

Crosfields' Mixed Choir, 1904. Choral singing was a popular leisure activity in the period before the First World War and this works choir provided a social alternative to the public house.

Warrington Male Choral Union Prize Choir, 1912. In harmony at last! — The Warrington Apollo Choir and the Warrington Male Voice Choir celebrated their first combined victory in a choral festival at Shrewsbury.

Parish Church day-trip to Southport in the 1920s. 'Oh, I do like to be beside the seaside!' — especially after a journey by bone-shaking charabanc at a maximum speed of twelve miles per hour.

Southport Pleasure Beach, 1909. More select than Blackpool, Southport still offered 'all the fun of the fair' — with a ride on the amazing Flying Machine — plus a chance to see the 'Mysterious Half Lady'.

Civic Sunday, 1914. Mayor Peter Peacock proudly surveys his new official vehicle from the steps of Warrington Town Hall.

Acknowledgements

Warrington Borough Council would like to thank all those who have made this volume possible and especially the photographers, the archivists (including Lever Bros. and Crosfields Chemicals) and members of the public who have generously donated and loaned prints to the Museum to help preserve the town's past for the future.